TOP 10

Written by Russell Ash
Illustrated by Pat McCarthy

The right of Russell Ash to be identified as Writer of this Work has been asserted
by him in accordance with the Copyright, Designs and Patents Act 1988

HENDERSON
PUBLISHING LTD

©1997 HENDERSON PUBLISHING LTD
TEXT COPYRIGHT © 1997 RUSSELL ASH

TOP 10

HIGHEST ACTIVE VOLCANOES IN THE WORLD

This list includes all volcanoes that have been active at some time during the 20th century.

	Volcano	Location	Latest activity	m	ft
1	Guallatiri	Chile	1987	6,060	19,882
2	Láscar	Chile	1991	5,990	19,652
3	Cotopaxi	Ecuador	1975	5,897	19,347
4	Tupungatito	Chile	1986	5,640	18,504
5	Popocatépetl	Mexico	1995	5,452	17,887
6	Ruiz	Colombia	1992	5,400	17,716
7	Sangay	Ecuador	1988	5,230	17,159
8	Guagua Pichincha	Ecuador	1988	4,784	15,696
9	Purace	Colombia	1977	4,755	15,601
10	Kliuchevskoi	Russia	1995	4,750	15,584

T O P 10

COLDEST INHABITED PLACES IN THE WORLD

	Location	Average temperature °C	°F
1	Norlísk, Russia	−10.9	12.4
2	Yakutsk, Russia	−10.1	13.8
3	Yellowknife, Canada	−5.4	22.3
4	Ulaanbator, Mongolia	−4.5	23.9
5	Fairbanks, Alaska, USA	−3.4	25.9
6	Surgut, Russia	−3.1	26.4
7	Chita, Russia	−2.7	27.1
8	Nizhnevartosvsk, Russia	−2.6	27.3
9	Hailar, Mongolia	−2.4	27.7
10	Bratsk, Russia	−2.2	28.0

HOTTEST INHABITED PLACES IN THE WORLD

	Location	Average temperature °C	°F
1	Djibouti, Djibouti	30.0	86.0
2=	Timbuktu, Mali	29.3	84.7
2=	Tirunelveli, India	29.3	84.7
2=	Tuticorin, India	29.3	84.7
5=	Nellore, India	29.2	84.6
5=	Santa Marta, Colombia	29.2	84.6
7=	Aden, South Yemen	28.9	84.0
7=	Madurai, India	28.9	84.0
7=	Niamey, Niger	28.9	84.0
10=	Hudaydah, North Yemen	28.8	83.8
10=	Ouagadougou, Burkina Faso	28.8	83.8
10=	Thanjāvūr, India	28.8	83.8
10=	Tiruchchlrāppalli, India	28.8	83.8

CRUCIAL TOP 10

TOP 10

MOST ENDANGERED MAMMALS IN THE WORLD

The first three mammals on the list have not been seen for many years and may well be extinct. However, zoologists are hopeful of the possibility of their survival.

	Mammal	Number
1=	Tasmanian wolf	?
1=	Halcon fruit bat	?
1=	Ghana fat mouse	?
4	Kouprey	10
5	Javan rhinoceros	50
6	Iriomote cat	60
7	Black lion tamarin	130
8	Pygmy hog	150
9	Tamaraw	200
10	Indus dolphin	400

SMALLEST MAMMALS

	Mammal	Weight g	oz	Length cm	in
1	Kitti's hognosed bat	2.0	0.07	2.9	1.1
2	Pygmy shrew	1.5	0.05	3.6	1.4
3	Pipistrelle bat	3.0	0.11	4.0	1.6
4	Little brown bat	8.0	0.28	4.0	1.6
5	Masked shrew	2.4	0.08	4.5	1.8
6	Southern blossom bat	12.0	0.42	5.0	2.0
7	Harvest mouse	5.0	0.18	5.8	2.3
8	Pygmy glider	12.0	0.42	6.0	2.4
9	House mouse	12.0	0.42	6.4	2.5
10	Common shrew	5.0	0.18	6.5	2.5

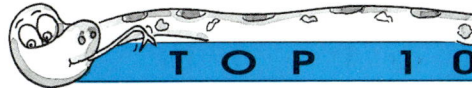

TOP 10

LONGEST SNAKES

	Snake	Maximum length m	ft
1	Reticulated python	10.7	35
2	Anaconda	8.5	28
3	Indian python	7.6	25
4	Diamond python	6.4	21
5	King cobra	5.8	19
6	Boa constrictor	4.9	16
7	Bushmaster	3.7	12
8	Giant brown snake	3.4	11
9	Diamondback rattlesnake	2.7	9
10	Indigo or gopher snake	2.4	8

DEADLIEST SNAKES IN THE WORLD

	Species	Native region
1=	Taipan	Australia and New Guinea
1=	Black mamba	Southern and Central Africa
3	Tiger snake	Australia
4	Common krait	South Asia
5	Death adder	Australia
6	Yellow or Cape cobra	Southern Africa
7	King cobra	India and Southeast Asia
8=	Bushmaster	Central and South America
8=	Green mamba	Africa
10	Coral snake	North, Central, and South America

Most people fear snakes, but only a few dozen of the 2,500-odd snake species that exist cause serious harm, and many more are beneficial because they prey on vermin.

TOP 10

LAZIEST ANIMALS IN THE WORLD

	Animal	Average hours of sleep
1	Koala	22
2	Sloth	20
3=	Armadillo	19
3=	Opossum	19
5	Lemur	16
6=	Hamster	14
6=	Squirrel	14
8=	Cat	13
8=	Pig	13
10	Spiny anteater	12

This list excludes periods of hibernation, which can last up to several months among creatures such as the ground squirrel, marmot, and brown bear.

FASTEST FISH IN THE WORLD

	Fish	Maximum recorded speed km/h	mph
1	Sailfish	110	68
2	Marlin	80	50
3	Bluefin tuna	74	46
4	Yellowfin tuna	70	44
5	Blue shark	69	43
6	Wahoo	66	41
7=	Bonefish	64	40
7=	Swordfish	64	40
9	Tarpon	56	35
10	Tiger shark	53	33

TOP 10

FASTEST MAMMALS IN THE WORLD

	Mammal	Maximum recorded speed km/h	mph
1	Cheetah	105	65
2	Pronghorn antelope	89	55
3=	Mongolian gazelle	80	50
3=	Springbok	80	50
5=	Grant's gazelle	76	47
5=	Thomson's gazelle	76	47
7	Brown hare	72	45
8	Horse	69	43
9=	Greyhound	68	42
9=	Red deer	68	42

T O P   1 0

FIRST TO GO OVER NIAGARA FALLS (AND SURVIVE)

	Name	Date	Method
1	Annie Edison Taylor	24 October 1901	Barrel
2	Bobby Leach	25 July 1911	Steel barrel
3	Jean Lussier	4 July 1928	Rubber ball fitted with oxygen cylinders
4	William Fitzgerald (aka Nathan Boya)	15 July 1961	Rubber ball
5	Karel Soucek	3 July 1984	Barrel
6	Steven Trotter	18 August 1985	Barrel
7	Dave Mundy	5 October 1985	Barrel
8=	Peter deBernardi	28 September 1989	Metal container
8=	Jeffrey Petkovich	28 September 1989	Metal container
10	Dave Mundy	26 September 1993	Diving bell

Source: Niagara Falls Museum

T O P   1 0

GIRLS' AND BOYS' NAMES IN THE UK

Girls		Boys
Jessica	**1**	Jack
Lauren	**2**	Daniel
Rebecca	**3**	Thomas
Sophie	**4**	James
Charlotte	**5**	Joshua
Hannah	**6**	Matthew
Amy	**7**	Ryan
Emily	**8**	Luke
Chloe	**9**	Samuel
Emma	**10**	Jordan

GIRLS' AND BOYS' NAMES IN THE US

Girls		Boys
Brittany	**1**	Michael
Ashley	**2**	Christopher
Jessica	**3**	Matthew
Amanda	**4**	Joshua
Sarah	**5**	Andrew
Megan	**6**	James
Caitlin	**7**	John
Samantha	**8**	Nicholas
Stephanie	**9**	Justin
Katherine	**10**	David

CRUCIAL TOP 10

TOP 10

LONGEST-REIGNING MONARCHS IN THE WORLD

	Monarch	Country	Reign	Age at accession	Years reigned
1	Louis XIV	France	1643–1715	5	72
2	John II	Liechtenstein	1858–1929	18	71
3	Franz-Josef	Austria–Hungary	1848–1916	18	67
4	Victoria	UK	1837–1901	18	63
5	Hirohito	Japan	1926–89	25	62
6	George III	UK	1760–1820	22	59
7	Louis XV	France	1715–74	5	59
8	Pedro II	Brazil	1831–89	6	58
9	Wilhelmina	Netherlands	1890–1948	10	58
10	Henry III	England	1216–72	9	56

T O P   1 0

MOST HIGHLY POPULATED CITIES IN THE WORLD

	City/country	Population
1	Tokyo–Yokohama, Japan	28,447,000
2	Mexico City, Mexico	23,913,000
3	São Paulo, Brazil	21,539,000
4	Seoul, South Korea	19,065,000
5	New York, USA	14,638,000
6	Osaka–Kobe–Kyoto, Japan	14,060,000
7	Bombay, India	13,532,000
8	Calcutta, India	12,885,000
9	Rio de Janeiro, Brazil	12,788,000
10	Buenos Aires, Argentina	12,232,000

SMALLEST COUNTRIES IN THE WORLD

	Area Country	sq km	sq miles
1	Vatican City	0.44	0.17
2	Monaco	1.81	0.7
3	Gibraltar	6.47	2.5
4	Macau	16.06	6.2
5	Nauru	21.23	8.2
6	Tuvalu	25.90	10.0
7	Bermuda	53.35	20.6
8	San Marino	59.57	23.0
9	Liechtenstein	157.99	61.0
10	Antigua	279.72	108.0

T O P   1 0

TALLEST HABITABLE BUILDINGS IN THE WORLD

	Building	Location	Year completed	Storeys	Height m.	ft
1	Petronas Towers	Kuala Lumpur, Malaysia	1996	96	452	1,482
2	Sears Tower *with spires*	Chicago, USA	1974	110	443 *520*	1,454 *1,707*
3	World Trade Center*	New York, USA	1973	110	417	1,368
4	Empire State Building *with spire*	New York, USA	1931	102	381 *449*	1,250 *1,472*
5	T & C Tower	Kao-hsiung, Taiwan	1997	85	348	1,142
6	Amoco Building	Chicago, USA	1973	80	346	1,136
7	John Hancock Center *with spire*	Chicago, USA	1968	100	344 *450*	1,127 *1,476*
8	Shun Hing Square *with spires*	Shenzen, China	1996	80	330 *384*	1,082 *1,263*
9	Sky Central Plaza *with spires*	Guangzhou, China	1996	80	323 *391*	1,060 *1,283*
10	Baiyoke II Tower	Bangkok, Thailand	1996	89	319	1,046

*Twin towers; the second tower, completed in 1973, has the same number of storeys but is slightly smaller at 415 m/1,362 ft – although its spire takes it up to 521 m/1,710 ft

TOP 10

LONGEST UNDERWATER TUNNELS IN THE WORLD

Tunnel	Location	Year completed	Length km	miles
1 Seikan (rail)	Japan	1988	53.90	33.49
2 Channel Tunnel (rail)	France/England	1994	49.94	31.03
3 Dai-Shimizu (rail)	Japan	1982	22.17	13.78
4 Shin-Kammon (rail)	Japan	1975	18.68	11.61
5 Severn (rail)	UK	1886	7.01	4.36
6 Haneda (rail)	Japan	1971	5.98	3.72
7 Kammon (rail)	Japan	1942	3.60	2.24
8 Kammon (road)	Japan	1958	3.46	2.15
9 Mersey (road)	UK	1934	3.43	2.13
10 Elbe (road)	Germany	1973	3.32	2.06

T O P 1 0

MOST WIDELY SPOKEN LANGUAGES IN THE WORLD

	Language	Approx. no. of speakers
1	Chinese (Mandarin)	931,000,000
2	English	463,000,000
3	Hindustani	400,000,000
4	Spanish	371,000,000
5	Russian	290,000,000
6	Arabic	215,000,000
7	Bengali	193,000,000
8	Portuguese	180,000,000
9	Malay-Indonesian	153,000,000
10	Japanese	126,000,000

COUNTRIES WITH THE MOST ENGLISH LANGUAGE SPEAKERS

	Country	Approx. no. of speakers
1	USA	224,900,000
2	UK	56,830,000
3	Canada	17,700,000
4	Australia	15,188,000
5	South Africa	3,620,000
6	Ireland	3,340,000
7	New Zealand	3,205,000
8	Jamaica	2,350,000
9	Trinidad & Tobago	1,200,000
10	Guyana	900,000

TOP 10

BEST-SELLING BRITISH COMICS OF ALL TIME

	Title	Published
1	*Beano*	1938–present
2	*Comic Cuts*	1890–1953
3	*Dandy*	1937–present
4	*Eagle*	1950–69; 1982–present
5	*Film Fun*	1920–62
6	*Illustrated Chips*	1890–1953
7	*Mickey Mouse Weekly*	1936–57
8	*Radio Fun*	1938–61
9	*Rainbow*	1914–56
10	*School Friend*	1950–65

BEST-SELLING CHILDREN'S BOOKS OF 1995 IN THE UK

	Title
1	*Pocahontas – Book of the Film*
2	*Eric Carle, The Very Hungry Caterpillar*
3	*Funfax Organiser*
4	*Caroline B. Cooney, Point Horror: Twins*
5	*Richard Carlisle and Lyn Weldon, Letterland ABC*
6	*The Lion King – Book of the Film*
7	*Terry Deary, Horrible Histories: The Blitzed Brits*
8	*Dick King-Smith, Babe*
9	*Terry Deary, Horrible Histories: Terrible Tudors*
10	*Nick Butterworth, After the Storm*

TOP 10

SINGLES OF THE 1990s IN THE US TO DATE*

	Title/artist	Year
1	*I Will Always Love You*, Whitney Houston	1992
2	*Whoomp! There It Is*, Tag Team	1993
3	*Everything I Do (I Do It for You)*, Bryan Adams	1991
4	*Gangsta's Paradise*, Coolio featuring LV	1995
5	*Baby Got Back*, Sir Mix-A-Lot	1992
6	*Vogue*, Madonna	1990
7	*End of the Road*, Boyz II Men	1992
8	*I'll Make Love to You*, Boyz II Men	1994
9	*I Swear*, All-4-One	1994
10	*Fantasy*, Mariah Carey	1995

*Up to 31 December 1995

TOP 10

SINGLES OF THE 1990s IN THE UK TO DATE*

	Title/artist	Year
1	*Unchained Melody*, Robson Green & Jerome Flynn	1995
2	*Love is All Around*, Wet Wet Wet	1994
3	*Everything I Do (I Do It for You)*, Bryan Adams	1991
4	*I Will Always Love You*, Whitney Houston	1992
5	*Gangsta's Paradise*, Coolio featuring LV	1995
6	*Think Twice*, Celine Dion	1994
7	*I Would Do Anything for Love (But I Won't Do That)*, Meat Loaf	1993
8	*I Believe/Up on the Roof*, Robson Green & Jerome Flynn	1995
9	*Back For Good*, Take That	1995
10	*Saturday Night*, Whigfield	1994

Up to 31 December 1995

TOP 10

SINGLES OF ALL TIME IN THE US

	Title/artist	Year
1	*White Christmas*, Bing Crosby	1942
2	*I Want to Hold Your Hand*, Beatles	1964
3	*Hound Dog/Don't Be Cruel*, Elvis Presley	1956
4	*It's Now or Never*, Elvis Presley	1960
5	*I Will Always Love You*, Whitney Houston	1992
6	*Hey Jude*, Beatles	1968
7	*We Are the World*, USA for Africa	1985
8	*Whoomp! There It Is*, Tag Team	1993
9	*Everything I Do (I Do It for You)*, Bryan Adams	1991
10	*The Chipmunk Song*, Chipmunks	1958

TOP 10

ALBUMS OF ALL TIME WORLDWIDE

	Artist	Album	Estimated sales
1	Michael Jackson	Thriller	40,000,000
2	Pink Floyd	Dark Side of the Moon	28,000,000
3	Meat Loaf	Bat Out of Hell	27,000,000
4	Soundtrack	The Bodyguard	26,000,000
5	Soundtrack	Saturday Night Fever	25,000,000
6=	Beatles	Sgt. Pepper's Lonely Hearts Club Band	24,000,000
6=	Eagles	Their Greatest Hits 1971–1975	24,000,000
8	Mariah Carey	Music Box	23,000,000
9=	Carole King	Tapestry	22,000,000
9=	Simon and Garfunkel	Bridge over Troubled Water	22,000,000
9=	Soundtrack	Grease	22,000,000
9=	Michael Jackson	Dangerous	22,000,000

TOP 10

POP MUSIC FILMS*

	Film	Year
1	The Blues Brothers	1980
2	Purple Rain	1984
3	La Bamba	1987
4	The Doors	1991
5	What's Love Got to Do With It	1993
6	Xanadu	1980
7	The Jazz Singer	1980
8	Sergeant Pepper's Lonely Hearts Club Band	1978
9	Lady Sings the Blues	1972
10	Pink Floyd – The Wall	1982

*The ranking is based on rental earnings of films in North America

HIGHEST-GROSSING FILMS OF 1995 IN THE WORLD

	Film	Box office gross ($)
1	Die Hard with a Vengeance	354,000,000
2	Batman Forever	333,000,000
3	Apollo 13	332,000,000
4	Pocahontas	318,000,000
5	Casper	280,000,000
6	Waterworld	255,000,000
7	Forrest Gump	207,000,000
8	Goldeneye	199,000,000
9	Outbreak	188,000,000
10	Dumb & Dumber	187,000,000

T O P   1 0

BIGGEST FILM FLOPS OF ALL TIME

	Film	Year	Estimated loss ($)
1	*Cutthroat Island*	1995	100,000,000
2	*The Adventures of Baron Münchhausen*	1988	48,100,000
3	*Ishtar*	1987	47,300,000
4	*Hudson Hawk*	1991	47,000,000
5	*Inchon*	1981	44,100,000
6	*The Cotton Club*	1984	38,100,000
7	*Santa Claus – The Movie*	1985	37,000,000
8	*Heaven's Gate*	1980	34,200,000
9	*Billy Bathgate*	1991	33,000,000
10	*Pirates*	1986	30,300,000

CRUCIAL TOP 10

TOP 10

MOST EXPENSIVE FILMS EVER MADE

	Film*	Year	Estimated cost ($)
1	Waterworld	1995	160,000,000
2	True Lies	1994	115,000,000
3	Cutthroat Island	1995	105,000,000
4	Inchon (US/Korea)	1981	102,000,000
5	War and Peace (USSR)	1967	100,000,000
6	Terminator 2: Judgment Day	1991	95,000,000
7	Total Recall	1990	85,000,000
8	The Last Action Hero	1993	82,500,000
9	Batman Returns	1992	80,000,000
10	Aliens[3]	1992	75,000,000

*All US-made unless otherwise stated

SCIENCE-FICTION AND FANTASY FILMS

1	E.T.: the Extra-Terrestrial	1982
2	Star Wars	1977
3	Return of the Jedi	1983
4	Batman	1989
5	The Empire Strikes Back	1980
6	Ghostbusters	1984
7	Terminator 2	1991
8	Back to the Future	1985
9	Batman Returns	1992
10	Ghost	1990

The first six films are also in the all-time Top 10, and all 10 are among the 21 most successful films ever, having earned over $80,000,000 each from North American rentals alone. Just outside this Top 10, another eight have had a rental income of over $60,000,000: *Close Encounters of the Third Kind*; *Gremlins*; *Honey, I Shrunk the Kids*; *Back to the Future, Part II*; *Teenage Mutant Ninja Turtles*; *Superman II*; *Total Recall*; and *Ghostbusters II*.

TOP 10

COMEDY FILMS

1	Forrest Gump	1994
2	Home Alone	1990
3	Mrs. Doubtfire	1993
4	Beverly Hills Cop	1984
5	Ghost	1990
6	Home Alone 2: Lost in New York	1992
7	Tootsie	1982
8	Pretty Woman	1990
9	Three Men and a Baby	1987
10	Beverly Hills Cop II	1987

FILMS TO WIN MOST OSCARS

	Film	Year	Awards
1	Ben-Hur	1959	11
2	West Side Story	1961	10
3=	Gigi	1958	9
3=	The Last Emperor	1987	9
5=	Gone with the Wind	1939	8
5=	From Here to Eternity	1953	8
5=	On the Waterfront	1954	8
5=	My Fair Lady	1964	8
5=	Cabaret	1972	8
5=	Gandhi	1982	8
5=	Amadeus	1984	8

CRUCIAL TOP 10

T O P   1 0

FIRST COUNTRIES TO HAVE TELEVISION*

	Country	Year
1	UK	1936
2	USA	1939
3	Former USSR	1939
4	France	1948
5	Brazil	1950
6	Cuba	1950
7	Mexico	1950
8	Argentina	1951
9	Denmark	1951
10	Netherlands	1951

*High-definition regular public broadcasting service

LONGEST-RUNNING PROGRAMMES ON BRITISH TELEVISION

	TV programme	First shown
1	*Panorama*	11 Nov 1953
2	*What the Papers Say*	5 Nov 1956
3	*The Sky at Night*	24 Apr 1957
4	*Grandstand*	11 Oct 1958
5	*Blue Peter*	16 Oct 1958
6	*Coronation Street*	9 Dec 1960
7	*Songs of Praise*	1 Oct 1961
8	*Top of the Pops*	1 Jan 1964
9	*Horizon*	2 May 1964
10	*Match of the Day*	22 Aug 1964

Only programmes appearing every year since their first screenings are listed in this Top 10.

TOP 10

TV AUDIENCES OF ALL TIME IN THE UK

	TV programme	Date	Audience
1	Royal Wedding of Prince Charles to Lady Diana Spencer	29 Jul 1981	39,000,000
2	Brazil vs. England, 1970 World Cup	10 Jun 1970	32,500,000
3=	England vs. West Germany, 1966 World Cup Final	30 Jul 1966	32,000,000
3=	Chelsea vs. Leeds, Cup Final Replay	28 Apr 1970	32,000,000
5	*EastEnders*, Christmas episode	26 Dec 1987	30,000,000
6	*Morecambe and Wise*, Christmas Show	25 Dec 1977	28,000,000
7=	World Heavyweight Boxing Championship: Joe Frazier vs. Cassius Clay	8 Mar 1971	27,000,000
7=	*Dallas* (episode revealing who shot J.R. Ewing)	22 Nov 1980	27,000,000
9	*To the Manor Born* (last episode)	11 Nov 1979	24,000,000
10	Torvill and Dean, Olympic Dance	21 Feb 1994	23,950,000

CRUCIAL TOP 10 25

T O P 1 0

BEST-SELLING CHILDREN'S VIDEOS OF 1995 IN THE US

1. *Land Before Time II: The Great Valley Adventure*
2. *Land Before Time III: The Time of the Great Giving*
3. *Sing Along Disney: The Lion King*
4. *Dr. Seuss/ How the Grinch Stole Christmas*
5. *Rudolph the Red-Nosed Reindeer*
6. *Barney: Imagination Island*
7. *Winnie the Pooh: And Christmas Too*
8. *Barney's Alphabet Zoo*
9. *Barney Live! In New York City*
10. *Barney: Families Are Special*

MOST RENTED VIDEOS OF 1995 IN THE UK

	Film	Approx. rentals
1	*Forrest Gump*	5,175,000
2	*Speed*	4,420,000
3	*Pulp Fiction*	4,390,000
4	*The Mask*	4,315,000
5	*True Lies*	4,100,000
6	*Stargate*	4,095,000
7	*The Specialist*	3,485,000
8	*Dumb and Dumber*	2,980,000
9	*Timecop*	2,650,000
10	*Four Weddings and a Funeral*	2,610,000

TOP 10

PROFESSIONS THAT WALK THE FURTHEST*

	Profession	Average walked per year	
		km	miles
1	Policeman/woman	2,626	1,632
2	Postman/woman	1,699	1,056
3	TV reporter	1,622	1,008
4	Nurse	1,516	942
5	Doctor	1,352	840
6	Shop assistant	1,294	804
7	Secretary	1,275	792
8	Actor	1,249	776
9	Public relations executive	1,072	666
10	Estate agent	1,001	622

*This list is based on professions in the US

TOP 10

HAMLEYS' BEST-SELLING TOYS AND GAMES IN 1995

1. Barbie (especially Butterfly Princess and Holiday Barbie)
2. Lego (especially Aquazone range)
3. Power Rangers figures
4. Sky Dancers (flying fairies)
5. Inline roller skates
6. Pogs and Pogmakers
7. Sega Lock-on (computer game)
8. Word Spin Scrabble (hand-held word game)
9. Bub-a-loo Bird (marionette)
10. Action Man

FIRST COUNTRIES & CITIES TO ISSUE POSTAGE STAMPS

	Country/city	Stamps issued
1	UK	May 1840
2	New York City, USA	Feb 1842
3	Zurich, Switzerland	Mar 1843
4	Brazil	Aug 1843
5	Geneva, Switzerland	Oct 1843
6	Basle, Switzerland	July 1845
7	USA	July 1847
8	Mauritius	Sep 1847
9	France	Jan 1849
10	Belgium	July 1849

TOP 10

MOST POPULAR FANCY-DRESS COSTUME STYLES IN THE UK*

Women		Men
Georgian	**1**	Cowboys
1920s	**2**	Cavaliers
Victorian	**3**	Rhett Butler (from *Gone with the Wind*)
Elizabethan	**4**	Georgian
Edwardian	**5**	Medieval
Showgirls	**6**	Roman soldiers
Western	**7**	1940s military/naval whites
1930s	**8**	Eastern/Indian
Far Eastern	**9**	Futuristic
1940s	**10**	Henley Regatta (striped blazer and boater)

*Based on loans by The Fancy Dress Emporium, a leading London costume-rental company

TOP 10

WORST RUBBISH PRODUCERS IN THE WORLD

	Country	Domestic waste per capita per annum	
		kg	lb
1	USA	721	1,590
2	Finland	624	1,376
3	Canada	601	1,325
4	Netherlands	497	1,096
5	Denmark	475	1,047
6	Norway	472	1,041
7	Hungary	463	1,021
8	Luxembourg	445	981
9	Switzerland	441	972
10	Japan	411	906

WORST DEFORESTING COUNTRIES IN THE WORLD

	Country	Average annual forest loss in 1980s (sq km)
1	Brazil	36,710
2	Indonesia	11,120
3	Zaïre	7,320
4	Mexico	6,780
5	Bolivia	6,250
6	Venezuela	5,990
7	Thailand	5,150
8	Sudan	4,820
9	Tanzania	4,380
10	Paraguay	4,030

During the 1980s the total loss of the Brazilian forest was equivalent to the entire area of Germany.

TOP 10

RICHEST PEOPLE IN THE WORLD*

	Name	Country	Business	Assets ($)
1	Bill Gates	USA	Computer software	14,800,000,000
2	Warren Buffett	USA	Textiles, etc.	9,200,000,000
3=	Hans Rausing	Sweden	Packaging	9,000,000,000
3=	Yoshiaki Tsutsumi	Japan	Property	9,000,000,000
5	Paul Sacher	Switzerland	Roche drug company	8,600,000,000
6	Tsai Wan-lin	Taiwan	Insurance	8,500,000,000
7=	Lee Shau Kee	Hong Kong	Property	6,500,000,000
7=	Kenneth T. Thomson	Canada	Publishing	6,500,000,000
9	Chung Ju-yung	Korea	Hyundai (cars)	6,200,000,000
10	Li Ka-shing	Hong Kong	Property, etc.	5,900,000,000

*Excluding royalty

Based on data published by Forbes Magazine

CRUCIAL TOP 10 31

T O P 1 0

HIGHEST-EARNING ENTERTAINERS IN THE WORLD*

	Entertainer	Profession	1994-95 income ($)
1	Steven Spielberg	Film producer/director	285,000,000
2	Oprah Winfrey	TV host/producer	146,000,000
3	David Copperfield	Illusionist	81,000,000
4	Andrew Lloyd Webber	Theatre producer/composer	48,000,000
5	Stephen King	Novelist/screenwriter	43,000,000
6=	Barney	Singer/dancer/children's educator	40,000,000
6=	Siegfried & Roy	Illusionists	40,000,000
8	Michael Crichton	Novelist	39,000,000
9	Robert Zemeckis	Film director	37,000,000
10	Charles M. Schulz	*Peanuts* cartoonist	36,000,000

*Other than actors and pop stars
Used by permission of Forbes Magazine

TOP 10

COUNTRIES WITH THE MOST DOLLAR BILLIONAIRES*

	Country	Billionaires
1	USA	129
2	Germany	48
3	Japan	34
4=	Hong Kong	12
4=	Thailand	12
6	France	11
7=	Indonesia	10
7=	Mexico	10
9=	Brazil	8
9=	Switzerland	8

*With a net worth of $1,000,000,000 or more
Based on data published in Forbes Magazine*

HIGHEST-EARNING DECEASED PEOPLE*

	Name	Year died
1	Elvis Presley	1977
2	John Lennon	1980
3	James Dean	1955
4	Jimi Hendrix	1970
5	Albert Einstein	1955
6	Marilyn Monroe	1962
7	Jim Morrison	1971
8	Humphrey Bogart	1957
9	Orson Welles	1985
10	Babe Ruth	1948

Earnings from royalties

T O P   1 0

RICHEST COUNTRIES IN THE WORLD

	Country	GDP per capita ($)
1	Switzerland	36,399
2	Luxembourg	35,583
3	Japan	31,451
4	Bermuda	28,293
5	Denmark	26,514
6	Norway	26,340
7	Sweden	24,833
8	USA	24,753
9	Iceland	23,985
10	Germany	23,561
	UK	*17,965*

POOREST COUNTRIES IN THE WORLD

	Country	GDP per capita ($)
1	Sudan	63
2	Somalia	78
3	Mozambique	81
4	Tanzania	94
5	Ethiopia	102
6	Afghanistan	111
7	Sierra Leone	145
8	Nepal	156
9	Bhutan	165
10	Vietnam	169

TOP 10

SWEET-CONSUMING NATIONS IN THE WORLD

	Country	Annual consumption (kg per head)		
		chocolate	other sweets	total
1	Netherlands	8.21	5.68	13.89
2	Denmark	6.91	6.39	13.30
3	Switzerland	10.03	2.90	12.93
4	UK	7.42	5.17	12.59
5	Belgium/Luxembourg	7.63	4.86	12.49
6	Ireland	6.65	5.78	12.43
7	Norway	7.89	4.37	12.26
8	Germany	6.57	5.68	12.25
9	Sweden	5.55	5.25	10.80
10	Austria	7.32	2.85	10.17
	USA	*4.66*	*3.44*	*8.10*

CANDY BRANDS IN THE US*

	Brand	Sales ($)*
1	M&M's	185,881,472
2	Brach's	181,870,852
3	Hershey	169,958,497
4	Reese's	152,339,870
5	Snickers	122,144,324
6	Hershey Kisses	119,178,840
7	Kit Kat	61,144,354
8	Butterfinger	51,361,624
9	Milky Way	48,005,216
10	Lifesavers	46,340,416

Sales through grocery stores during 1993 – total sales of some brands through drugstores and other outlets may more than double these figures

T O P   1 0

OLDEST-ESTABLISHED BRITISH CHOCOLATE PRODUCTS

	Product	Year introduced
1	Fry's Chocolate Cream	1866
2	Cadbury's Dairy Milk	1905
3	Cadbury's Bournville	1908
4	Fry's Turkish Delight	1914
5	Cadbury's Milk Tray	1915
6	Cadbury's Creme Egg	1920
7=	Cadbury's Fruit & Nut	1921
7=	Terry's 1767 Bitter Bar	1921
9	Terry's Neapolitan	1922
10	Terry's Spartan	1923

CHOCOLATE LOVERS

Cocoa was drunk by the Aztecs and was taken from South America to Spain in the 16th century. Sugar was added to make the bitter cocoa more palatable, then milk to create chocolate. The diarist Samuel Pepys recorded his first drink of "jocolatte" on 24 November 1664. In Britain the industry came under the control of three Quaker families, Fry, Rowntree and Cadbury who encouraged drinking cocoa or chocolate as an alternative to alcohol.

TOP 10

ICE CREAM CONSUMING COUNTRIES IN THE WORLD

	Country	Production per capita litres	pints
1	USA	22.26	39.18
2	New Zealand	17.84	31.40
3	Denmark	17.04	29.99
4	Australia	15.45	27.19
5	Belgium/Luxembourg	14.91	26.24
6	Sweden	14.24	25.06
7	Canada	12.79	22.51
8	Norway	12.14	21.37
9	Ireland	9.14	16.09
10	Switzerland	7.47	13.15

CALORIE-CONSUMING COUNTRIES IN THE WORLD

	Country	Average daily consumption per capita
1	Ireland	3,847
2	Greece	3,815
3	Cyprus	3,779
4	USA	3,732
5	Spain	3,708
6	Belgium/Luxembourg	3,681
7	New Zealand	3,669
8	Denmark	3,664
9	Portugal	3,634
10	France	3,633
	UK	*3,317*
	World average	*2,718*

TOP 10

SUGAR-CONSUMING COUNTRIES IN THE WORLD

	Country	Annual consumption per capita	
		kg	lb
1	Swaziland	169.5	373.7
2	Singapore	79.8	175.9
3	Belize	62.6	138.0
4	Australia	61.2	134.9
5	Cuba	60.5	133.4
6	Iceland	60.2	132.7
7	Israel	57.7	127.2
8	Denmark	57.6	127.0
9	Barbados	57.5	126.8
10	Costa Rica	57.4	126.5
	UK	*43.7*	*96.3*
	US	*28.9*	*63.7*

TOP 10

MILK-DRINKING COUNTRIES IN THE WORLD

	Country*	Annual consumption per capita	
		litres	pints
1	Iceland	174.2	306.6
2	Finland	165.1	290.6
3	Norway	142.9	251.5
4	Sweden	122.5	215.6
5	Spain	111.6	196.4
6	UK	111.5	196.2
7	Denmark	111.3	195.9
8	Switzerland	98.3	173.0
9	New Zealand	97.9	172.3
10	Australia	95.6	168.3

Those reporting to the International Dairy Federation only

SOFT-DRINK CONSUMERS IN THE WORLD

	Country	Annual consumption per capita	
		litres	pints
1	Switzerland	105.0	184.8
2	Barbados	81.4	143.2
3	Bahamas	75.0	132.0
4	USA	74.7	131.5
5	Australia	73.9	130.0
6	Germany	72.0	126.7
7	Canada	69.3	122.0
8=	Belgium	65.0	114.4
8=	Japan	65.0	114.4
10	Singapore	61.4	108.1
	UK	39.0	68.6

CRUCIAL TOP 10

T O P   1 0

BEST-SELLING CARS OF ALL TIME

	Model/ year first produced	Estimated no. made
1	Volkswagen Beetle, 1937*	21,220,000
2	Toyota Corolla, 1963	20,000,000
3	Ford Model T, 1908	15,007,033
4	Volkswagen Golf, 1974	14,800,000
5	Lada Riva, 1970	13,500,000
6	Ford Escort/Orion, 1967	12,000,000
7	Nissan Sunny/Pulsar, 1966	10,200,000
8	Mazda 323, 1977	9,500,000
9	Renault 4, 1961	8,100,000
10	Honda Civic, 1972	8,000,000

Still produced in Mexico and Brazil

COUNTRIES WITH THE MOST AIRPORTS

	Country	Airports
1	USA	15,032
2	Brazil	3,467
3	Russia	2,517
4	Mexico	2,055
5	Argentina	1,602
6	Canada	1,386
7	Bolivia	1,382
8	Colombia	1,307
9	Paraguay	929
10	South Africa	853

TOP 10

AMUSEMENT AND THEME PARKS IN THE WORLD

	Park/location	Estimated visitors (1995)
1	Tokyo Disneyland, Tokyo, Japan	15,509,000
2	Disneyland, California, USA	14,100,000
3	Magic Kingdom at Walt Disney World, Florida, USA	12,900,000
4=	EuroDisney, Marne-la-Vallée, France	10,700,000
4=	EPCOT at Walt Disney World, Florida, USA	10,700,000
6	Disney-MGM Studios Theme Park at Walt Disney World, Florida, USA	9,500,000
7	Universal Studios Florida, Florida, USA	8,000,000
8	Yong-In Farmland, Kyonggi-Do, South Korea	7,300,000
9	Blackpool Pleasure Beach, Blackpool, UK	7,200,000
10	Yokohama Hakkeijima Sea Paradise, Japan	6,000,000

Source: Amusement Business

CRUCIAL TOP 10 41

TOP 10

LONDON TOURIST ATTRACTIONS

	Attraction	Visitors (1995)
1	British Museum	5,745,866
2	National Gallery	4,469,019
3	Madame Tussaud's	2,703,283
4	Tower of London	2,536,680
5	Funland and Laserbowl, Trocadero	2,500,000
6	Westminster Abbey	2,245,000
7	St. Paul's Cathedral	2,220,000
8	Tate Gallery	1,769,662
9	Science Museum	1,556,368
10	Victoria & Albert Museum	1,224,030

T O P 1 0

SUMMER OLYMPICS WITH THE MOST COMPETITORS

	Country	Year	Competing countries	Competitors
1	Atlanta	1996	197	10,700
2	Barcelona	1992	172	9,369
3	Seoul	1988	159	9,101
4	Munich	1972	122	7,156
5	Los Angeles	1984	141	7,058
6	Montreal	1976	92	6,085
7	Mexico City	1968	112	5,530
8	Rome	1960	83	5,346
9	Moscow	1980	81	5,326
10	Tokyo	1964	93	5,140

BASEBALL TEAMS WITH THE MOST WORLD SERIES WINS

	Team*	Wins
1	New York Yankees	22
2=	Philadelphia/Kansas City/Oakland Athletics	9
2=	St. Louis Cardinals	9
4	Brooklyn/Los Angeles Dodgers	6
5=	Boston Red Sox	5
5=	Cincinnati Reds	5
5=	New York/San Francisco Giants	5
5=	Pittsburgh Pirates	5
9	Detroit Tigers	4
10=	St. Louis/Baltimore Orioles	3
10=	Washington Senators/Minnesota Twins	3

*Teams separated by / indicate changes of franchise and are regarded as the same team for Major League record purposes

TOP 10

CRICKET PLAYERS WITH THE MOST TEST APPEARANCES

	Player/country	Years	Tests*
1	Allan Border (Australia)	1978–94	156
2	Kapil Dev (India)	1978–94	131
3	Sunil Gavaskar (India)	1971–87	125
4	Javed Miandad (Pakistan)	1976–94	124
5	Viv Richards (West Indies)	1974–91	121
6	Graham Gooch (England)	1975–95	118
7	David Gower (England)	1978–92	117
8=	Dilip Vengsarkar (India)	1976–92	116
8=	Desmond Haynes (West Indies)	1978–94	116
10	Colin Cowdrey (England)	1954–75	114

*To 30 January 1996

TOP 10

MOST SUCCESSFUL AMERICAN FOOTBALL TEAMS*

Team		**Wins**	**Runners-up**	**Points**
1	Dallas Cowboys	4	3	11
2	San Francisco 49ers	5	0	10
3	Pittsburgh Steelers	4	1	9
4	Washington Redskins	3	2	8
5=	Oakland/Los Angeles Raiders	3	1	7
5=	Miami Dolphins	2	3	7
7=	Green Bay Packers	2	0	4
7=	New York Giants	2	0	4
9=	Buffalo Bills	0	4	4
9=	Denver Broncos	0	4	4
9=	Minnesota Vikings	0	4	4

*Based on two points for a Super Bowl win, and one for runner-up

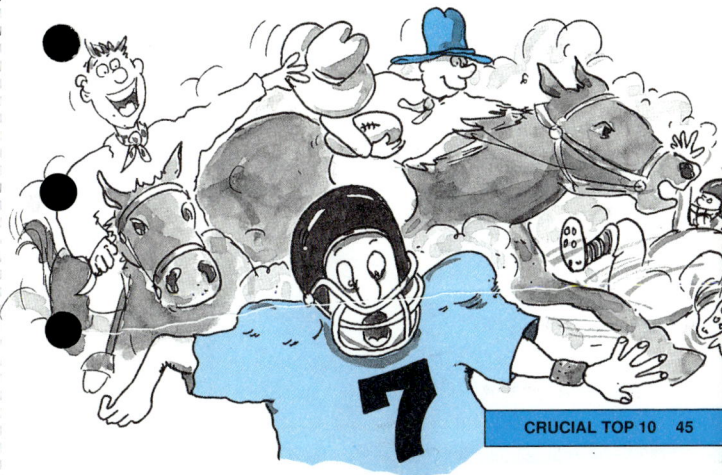

TOP 10

MOTOR RACING DRIVERS WITH THE MOST WORLD TITLES (FORMULA ONE)

	Driver/nationality	Titles
1	Juan Manuel Fangio (Argentina)	5
2	Alain Prost (France)	4
3=	Jack Brabham (Australia)	3
3=	Niki Lauda (Austria)	3
3=	Nelson Piquet (Brazil)	3
3=	Ayrton Senna (Brazil)	3
3=	Jackie Stewart (UK)	3
8=	Alberto Ascari (Italy)	2
8=	Jim Clark (UK)	2
8=	Graham Hill (UK)	2
8=	Emerson Fittipaldi (Brazil)	2
8=	Michael Schumacher (Germany)	2

MOTOR RACING MANUFACTURERS WITH THE MOST WORLD TITLES

	Manufacturer	**Titles**
1	Ferrari	8
2=	Lotus	7
2=	Williams	7
4	McLaren	6
5=	Brabham	2
5=	Cooper	2

	Manufacturer	**Titles**
7=	BRM	1
7=	Matra	1
7=	Tyrrell	1
7=	Vanwall	1
7=	Benetton	1

TOP 10

OLDEST UK FOOTBALL LEAGUE CLUBS

	Club	Year formed
1	Notts County	1862
2	Stoke City	1863
3	Nottingham Forest	1865
4	Chesterfield	1866
5	Sheffield Wednesday	1867
6	Reading	1871
7	Wrexham	1873
8=	Aston Villa	1874
8=	Bolton Wanderers	1874
10=	Birmingham City	1875
10=	Blackburn Rovers	1875

UK FOOTBALL CLUBS WITH THE MOST BRITISH TITLES

	Team	League Titles	FA Cup	League Cup	Total
1	Glasgow Rangers	45	26	19	90
2	Glasgow Celtic	35	30	9	74
3	Liverpool	18	4	5	27
4=	Arsenal	10	6	2	18
4=	Aston Villa	7	7	4	18
4=	Manchester United	9	8	1	18
7	Aberdeen	4	7	4	15
8	Everton	9	5	-	14
9	Heart of Midlothian	4	5	4	13
10	Tottenham Hotspur	2	8	2	12

TOP 10

HIGHEST-EARNING SPORTSMEN IN THE WORLD IN 1995

	Name*	Sport	Salary/winnings	Income ($) Other#	Total
1	Michael Jordan	Basketball	3,900,000	40,000,000	43,900,000
2	Mike Tyson	Boxing	40,000,000	-	40,000,000
3	Deion Sanders	Football/Baseball	16,500,000	6,000,000	22,500,000
4	Riddick Bowe	Boxing	22,000,000	200,000	22,200,000
5	Shaquille O'Neal	Basketball	4,900,000	17,000,000	21,900,000
6	George Foreman	Boxing	10,000,000	8,000,000	18,000,000
7	Andre Agassi	Tennis	3,000,000	13,000,000	16,000,000
8	Jack Nicklaus	Golf	600,000	14,500,000	15,100,000
9	Michael Schumacher (Germany)	Motor racing	10,000,000	5,000,000	15,000,000
10	Wayne Gretzky (Canada)	Ice hockey	8,500,000	6,000,000	14,500,000

*All sportsmen are from the US, unless otherwise stated
#Sponsorship and royalty income from endorsed sporting products

Used by permission of Forbes Magazine